IMAGES
of America

CHAMPLAIN

This image of the Champlain boatyard at the foot of River Street depicts two boats under construction. Many barges, canal boats, and private boats were constructed at this location over the years.

On the cover: Here a gentleman waters down the dirt on Main Street in Champlain. This *c.* 1900 photograph captures the canopy of elm trees that once covered the street. When asked their favorite memory of the "old" days in Champlain, most residents recall the image of a graceful, tree-lined Main Street. (Courtesy Special Collections, Feinberg Library, Plattsburgh State University.)

IMAGES
of America

CHAMPLAIN

Kimberly J. Lamay
and Celine Racine Paquette

ARCADIA
PUBLISHING

Published by Arcadia Publishing
Charleston, South Carolina

Library of Congress Catalog Card Number: 2006924316

For all general information contact Arcadia Publishing at:
Telephone 843-853-2070
Fax 843-853-0044
E-mail sales@arcadiapublishing.com
For customer service and orders:
Toll-Free 1-888-313-2665

Visit us on the Internet at www.arcadiapublishing.com

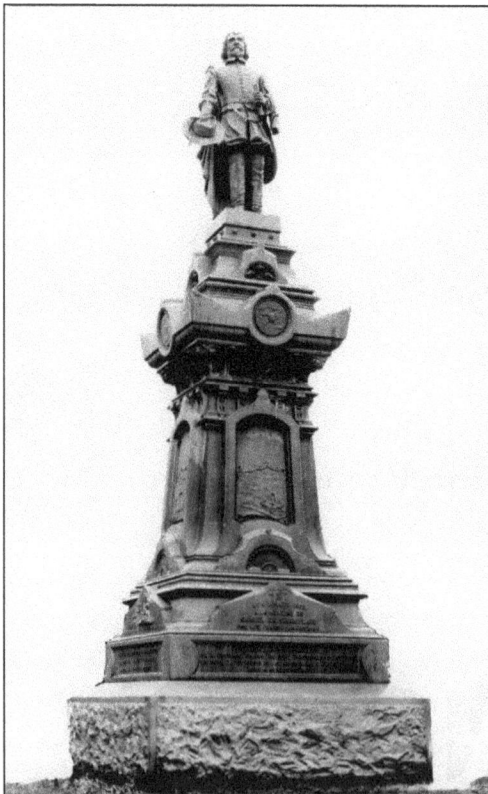

The town and village of Champlain are named for French explorer Samuel de Champlain. This monument to Champlain was installed in front of St. Mary's Church in 1907. An inscription at the base of the monument calls Champlain a "fervent Christian; an intrepid navigator; a man of letters and the discoverer of the gem of the lakes of America."

CONTENTS

ACKNOWLEDGMENTS

We are extremely grateful to the following people who generously provided photographs, anecdotes, and encouragement: Gloria Ashline, Isabel and Jerry Ashline, Lawrence Ashline, Richard and Marie Ashline, Leeward Babbie, Louis and Rita Bedard, Delia Bertrand, Calvin Castine, Florence Cardin, Janet Carey, Louise Chevalier, Lockwood Clark Sr., Lockwood Clark Jr., Emmet Dame, Roxanne Downs, William and Agatha Dubois, Mary Gordon, Alan Kaufman, Kurt Kaufman, James Kennedy, Bruce LaBelle, William LaBelle, Carl Lafontaine, Michael and Pat Lafontaine, Lucienne Lafountain, Jane and Lee Laplante, Francis Laurin, Rita Rae Laurin, Richard and Sharron Laventure, Joyce Lavoie, Susan and Jack Mawhinney, Marshall Maynard, Gerald Mayo, Albert and Ione Morelli, David Patrick, Donald Phaneuf, Doris Picard, Christine Racine, James Rochester, John and Joanne Southwick, Rita Stone, Theresa Trombly, Chris Trombley, Anna Trow, Theresa Venne, Jane West, and Kristi and Scott Yelle.

We are especially indebted to the helpful staff at SUNY Plattsburgh. Many images were provided at the courtesy of Special Collections, Feinberg Library, Plattsburgh State University.

This publication depended very much on the cooperation of past and present citizens of Champlain. Your generosity, guidance, and support made this book possible.

INTRODUCTION

Champlain has a rich history dating back to its permanent settlement right after the Revolutionary War. Soldiers fresh from a victory over the British were given bounty land grants for service to their country. Many of these soldiers were Canadian refugees who migrated south to aid in the defeat of England. Most soldiers sold their land grants because of the remote, unsettled location, but a few hardy souls accepted the challenge of this new frontier and established Champlain.

The War of 1812 followed quickly on the heels of the Revolutionary War, and the new town found itself on the front lines of battle. As early as 1807, when war seemed inevitable, the governor authorized the delivery of arms and ammunition for use by the citizens. Residents endured raids, occupation, and the constant threat of violence at their doorstep until the peace celebration in February 1815.

Champlain was also, surprisingly, on the front lines for the Civil War. Few people are aware of the threat posed by Confederate troops that amassed in Montreal in the last years of the war. Desperate for a way to distract Gen. Ulysses S. Grant and his troops on their march through the South, Gen. Robert E. Lee created a unit of rebel soldiers from a motley crew of mercenaries and escapees from northern prison camps. Their one successful raid, on St. Albans, Vermont, in October 1864, led to the creation of home guards along the northern border from Maine to Ohio. Champlain created a guard with over 100 men, many of whom were community and business leaders, to guard against rebel incursions.

Wars, floods, and other disasters have tested the mettle of residents, and prosperity has come and gone from Champlain more than once as the town struggled through the depths of the 1873 financial panic and the Depression in the 1930s. The town has seen the slow erosion of its agricultural economy, and the village has suffered through the loss of major employers that had served the community for many generations.

In 1931, during the height of the Depression, a local paper reprinted an article to remind citizens that every community goes through a cycle of ups and downs. The article was originally published in 1882 in the *Champlain Interview and Rouses Point Star*. It starts out by proclaiming, "too many people undertake to assume that Champlain is dead, as a place of business and social importance. Some of these [people] have honestly judged it by its condition during the years of widespread financial distress; . . . while many of our own people are actually responsible for a good share of whatever reputation for dullness their town suffers at home and abroad." The writer goes on to say, "to those who believe that Champlain is dead, we say, look at the map; look at her soil and natural resources; consider her manifest advantages of location and wealth." "(Champlain is) by nature a wealthy town."

His words are as true today as they were in 1882, and few places can boast either such a prime location or such a storied past. Champlain's historic heritage should be a point of pride for the community. Hopefully this book will encourage people to seek out and preserve the objects, structures, and places that tell Champlain's story. While there are still many beautiful, historic buildings in Champlain, so many others have been, or are about to be, lost forever. And while many community residents have held onto the photographs they shared with us for this publication, many other photographs and pieces of the past have been relegated to musty attics, or worse, the garbage bin.

It is hoped that these images depicting Champlain's colorful and robust history might inspire efforts to preserve the Champlain of the past and build the Champlain of the future.

All royalties from the sale of this book are being donated to the Samuel de Champlain Historic Society in furtherance of the local history center being developed in the former bank building. The center will be a repository for books, documents, and artifacts relevant to Champlain's history.

One

PEOPLE AND PASTIMES

Champlain's earliest history rests squarely on the shoulders of founding father Pliny Moore. In 1776, at the age of 17, Moore enlisted in the army and served honorably in a number of campaigns in the Revolutionary War. After the war, he acquired the 11,600-acre Smith and Graves Patent (also called the Moorsfield Patent) and settled in Champlain with several other intrepid town pioneers. Moore was the first postmaster of Champlain and the first judge of common pleas in Clinton County.

Other individuals who have made their mark on Champlain include Freeman and Bartlett Nye, brothers who settled in Champlain in 1807. The Nyes were highly successful businessmen who owned many buildings in the town and village. Another set of brothers, Timothy and George Hoyle, came to prominence in the mid-19th century. Timothy was the first president of the village, and both he and his brother George served in the New York State Assembly.

Dr. William Beaumont and Jehudi Ashmun brought national and international acclaim to Champlain. Beaumont was the village's first schoolmaster, serving from 1807 to 1810. After studying with a local doctor, he joined the U.S. Army and eventually became a post surgeon. While on the job in Michigan, one of his patients was afflicted with an open stomach wound that never healed. Beaumont conducted numerous experiments by inserting different food items directly in the stomach opening. His research formed the basis for much of what we know of the digestive system today. Ashmun's dedicated work with a colony of former slaves in Africa brought him international acclaim as "the Father of Liberia." Ashmun, who was born and raised in Champlain, dedicated the final years of his short life to stabilizing the first independent republic founded by freed American slaves in 1847.

More recently, architect Hugh McLellan, a descendant of Pliny Moore, conducted a 50-year transcription and preservation project of Moore's letters and documents detailing Champlain's early history. Together with his son Woody, they preserved and reprinted many documents that have contributed greatly to our understanding of the town's history.

Pliny Moore, born on April 14, 1759, served in several regiments during the Revolutionary War and received a bounty of land called the Smith and Graves Patent. The patent encompasses what is now the town of Champlain. In May 1789, he permanently settled in Champlain and built his home on the banks of the Great Chazy River (today the site of the Clark Funeral Home). Moore was an accomplished man who served in several town offices and operated sawmills and textile mills on both sides of the border before his death on August 18, 1822.

Capt. Antoine Paulint was an officer with Moses Hazen's regiment during the Revolutionary War. Captain Paulint had been one of many Canadians to take up arms against the British at the start of the war. Commander Hazen is credited with ensuring that his men, many of whom were Canadian refugees, received frontier land grants at the close of the war as a reward for service. One such land grant was given to Captain Paulint, who settled in Corbeau (now Coopersville) with his family.

Bartlett Nye, a Mayflower descendant, was
born in Massachusetts in 1799. Bartlett and
his older brother Freeman Nye established
F&B Nye and operated sawmills and farms
on both sides of the U.S.-Canadian border.
In addition to owning many buildings
in the village and town, Bartlett built a
mansion on the corner of Elm and Prospect
Streets, known as Locust Hill (later to
become the Savoy Hotel).

Two women converse on the corner of Oak and Main Streets in this c. 1900 photograph. Note
the hitching post and step, for those arriving by horse or carriage.

Orin Southwick and Frances Stewart pose on June 29, 1898, their wedding day. Orin Southwick, born in 1870, was a cofounder of the Champlain Telephone Company. He died in 1966 at the age of 96. The couple is surrounded by, from left to right, Edward Southwick, Mac Stewart, Lois Perry, Katherine Stewart, unidentified, and Charles Stewart. The photograph was taken at the Stewart farmhouse.

The Southwick family celebrates Thanksgiving in their farmhouse on Southwick Road in this 1901 photograph. From left to right are Orin Southwick, Frances Stewart, Marion Southwick, Katherine Stewart, Charles Southwick, Mrs. Southwick, and Edward Southwick.

Emma Garrand is one of the women in this group celebrating Easter Sunday in 1904. The photograph was taken in front of a sugar shack in Perry's Mills.

Alfred Bredenberg was born in Sweden and came to the United States at an early age. He started out working in New York City where he had plans for a new bookbinding machine. He was soon hired by the T. W. and C. B. Sheridan Company of New York and sent to Champlain. He is considered the father of high-speed bookbinding for his inventions while working for Sheridan in Champlain.

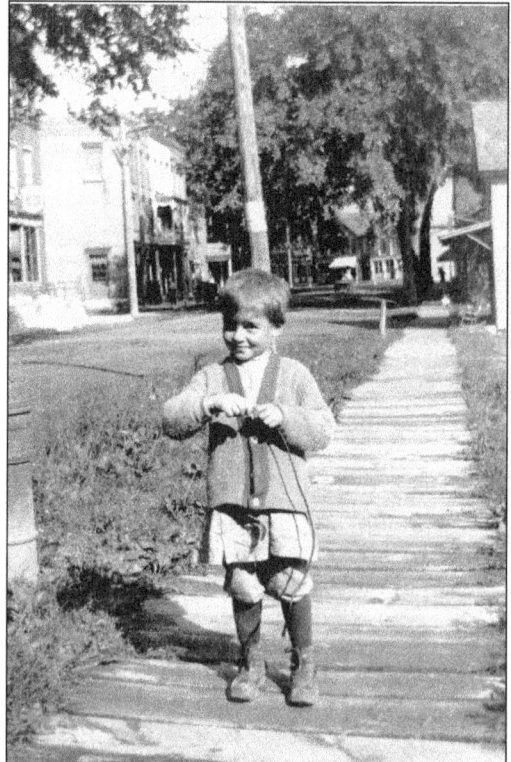

This image from Marion Ashline's photo album is captioned, "On the Boardwalk." Wooden sidewalks like this one along Main Street were part of the village landscape in the late 19th century. Until 1895, residents were responsible for constructing and maintaining the sidewalks in front of their homes.

This 1885 group photograph was taken in Jerome Barney's Perry's Mills photograph studio. From left to right are (first row) Achsah Bateman, Louise Southwick, and Orin Southwick; (second row) Abbie Hutchins (?), Louise Stone, Rachel Bateman, Marion Southwick, Blanche Gardner, and Eve Letson.

Nancy Gorbett Forsyth (seated), wife of James Forsyth, is surrounded by her family in this *c.* 1880 photograph. The family is at the Forsyth homestead in King's Bay. She is the great-great-grandmother of Carl, Reginald, Beatrice, and Michael LaFontaine.

Mrs. Frank Jefferson, Mrs. Pierre Lariviere, and Margaret Paquette (from left to right) pose for this photograph in their Victorian finery. The Paquettes ran a tourist home out of their house on Main Street. Members of the New York City Athletic Club, many of whom were very affluent, would visit the guest home to spend some time in the country. Margaret Paquette handled all the cooking, and William Paquette would take his guests musky fishing.

In this photograph, Charles Langvein, husband of Sarah LaValley, stands in front of the Champlain railroad station.

Three unidentified people enjoy a ride on the Great Chazy River on a boat christened *JoJo*. The Great Chazy River was a famous location for musky fishing.

In this photograph, Pierre Lariviere and party head for the mouth of the river.

A crowd gathers along the edge of a baseball field in this 1913 photograph. Lifelong resident Bill LaBelle remembers the field, located on Elm Street, was known as "Nye Athletic Field." LaBelle is now 98 years old.

Hector Kaufman sits in the driver's seat of this Model T car with two unidentified individuals.

Bill Earl's bicycle repair shop was a popular hang out for village boys. Earl charged youngsters according to what they could pay and, more often than not, did repairs free of charge. He often accompanied many of his young friends on bike rides around the countryside and on adventures in Canada and on the islands of Lake Champlain. Earl was so beloved that upon his death at 76 in 1943, a tribute was sent out to the *North Countryman* in his memory signed, "The Sons of Honest Bill." The tribute included this passage: "It was Bill who gave us our first boat ride on the river, and Bill taught us to ride a bike. And it was Bill, too who provided the opportunity to earn a little money for the cowboy show at the theatre – and he showed us how to make things of wood, such as boats and windmills and the like. He was the friend of everybody, particularly the children. We can see him again, this Uncle Bill, as he rode about the pleasant countryside with his pals – a dozen or more boys strung out in a line behind him on their bikes. . .. And there were tales of his father's sawmill on the bank of the river, of the old tannery, the shirt factory and the brickyards, and of how the machine shop was used to repair locomotives in the early days of the railroad."

This photograph shows Bill Earl embarking on a boat adventure with a young follower.

Louis C. Lafontaine was appointed by the governor as a member of the Lake Champlain Tercentenary Commission in 1908. He assisted with planning the public celebration of the 300th anniversary of Lake Champlain's discovery by Samuel de Champlain. Lafontaine was also a principal planner for the installation of the monument to Samuel de Champlain at St. Mary's Church. Currently, planning is underway for the 400th anniversary celebration of explorer Champlain's July 1609 expedition.

T. W. and C. B. Sheridan acquired an interest in the Champlain Foundry and Machine Shop in 1887 and became full owners a short time later. T. W. Sheridan is pictured in this undated image.

Hugh McLellan (left) and Eldridge Moore pose in this 1952 image. McLellan, born in 1874, was the great-great-grandson of Pliny Moore. In 1915, he started the transcription and preservation of the Pliny Moore papers dealing with Champlain's early history. Hugh and his son Woody printed many volumes of historical material with his Moorsfield Press.

A uniformed police officer stands near a traffic dummy on Main Street in this *c.* 1915 photograph. The sign reads, "Village of Champlain, Caution: Keep right; Use Texaco." Three Model T cars are parked along the street behind the officer.

Oscar and Henrik Bredenberg were two brothers who started a ski manufacturing business in Champlain around 1915. This photograph is labeled simply "Bredenberg 12." It may have been taken at the Bredenberg residence on Oak Street.

Alfred Babbie (left) and William Paquette man the counter at Ralph Lewis's hardware store in this 1920s photograph. Ingersoll Yankee pocket watches are being sold on a counter display for $1.50 each.

The postmistress Margaret Senecal is standing second from the left in this *c.* 1930 photograph of the interior of the post office. Her sister, Grace Senecal, is in the middle.

From left to right, Katherine (Falcon) Glaude, Frances Jeanette Falcon, and Mary Grace Falcon bundle up against a North Country winter around 1928.

The Nye family sits on their Locust Hill porch in this September 1898 photograph. From left to right are Charles, Laura, Grace, and Elsie Nye, and Malcolm McLellan. Laura Nye was the wife of Bartlett Nye, the builder of Locust Hill. In the 1930s, the mansion was converted into the Savoy Hotel.

In 1938, the New York State education department erected this cast-iron marker commemorating the birthplace of Jehudi Ashmun, who is known as the founder of Liberia. The marker, on Canada Street (now Meridian Road), was dedicated as part of the sesquicentennial celebration in Champlain that year. Ashmun was born in 1794 on Oak Street and went on to become one of Champlain's most famous sons. After teaching school in Champlain, Ashmun moved to the Washington, D.C., area where he worked with the American Colonization Society to establish a colony in Liberia for former African slaves. Ashmun and his wife moved to Liberia in 1822, and he stayed for six years attempting to stabilize the fledging colony and establish a democratic government. He has been heralded as "the Father of Liberia."

Fernand Leger, an acclaimed cubist artist who painted in the style of Picasso, lived in Champlain on and off during World War II. He left France around the time of the Nazi occupation, as Hitler began to place limitations on the arts community. Leger and Madame Roux lived in a house on the golf course road owned by Mrs. Trombly. This photograph was taken by Hugh McLellan near his printing office in Champlain. The Pliny Moore homestead is in the background. An exhibition catalog of Leger's work produced in 1982 noted that he was probably captivated by the green orchards and French-speaking residents in Champlain, both of which must have reminded him of Normandy.

Five of Champlain's prettiest residents linger on the Main Street bridge in the 1940s. From left to right, Jeanne LaFountaine, Agatha Babbie, Margaret Jordan, Rita Dubois, and Martha Trombley were close friends who loved to walk around the village and talk about the day's events.

Champlain ladies enjoy a night out at Au Lutin Restaurant in Montreal in November 1945. The restaurant was known for letting patrons feed a baby pig as part of their dining experience. From left to right are Vanita Maher, Frances St. Maxens, Helen Tudhope, Jesse Codding (feeding pig), and Annie Southwick.

Two

HOMESTEADS

A residential town with all of the popular and most coveted features of the beautiful villages in northern New York, it is especially noted for its fine houses, its home sites set off in gardens [with] wide avenues and well shaded thoroughfares . . . Its population is somewhat cosmopolitan, but the French and American families are in the majority. It was incorporated in 1873 and is one of the best governed little villages in Northern New York. Its inhabitants are intensely loyal, its business men enterprising and up-to-date and its village officers progressive.

So reported William Allen in a 1910 newspaper article titled "Beautiful Champlain." Champlain has retained many of the fine old homes that Allen applauds, and they continue to be a point of community pride. A casual observer may not notice the wealth of fine homes in the area as many are located just off Main Street where local businessmen took advantage of higher terrain to garner better views of the village. From these stately structures on Oak Street, to the farmhouses that dot the countryside, Champlain's residences represent all the architectural styles typical of the last century.

Some of the more notable structures include the Moore stone farmhouse and Dewey Tavern in the town, and the Whiteside home on Oak Street in the village. The Moore farmhouse, which dates from 1808, is known as the oldest house in Champlain. Located on Prospect Street, modern siding covers the original stone structure that was built by Champlain founder Pliny Moore. Dewey Tavern, built in 1800, has a storied past dating back to the War of 1812. The 15-room tavern and inn served as lodging for both American and British officers as the battle lines continually changed. The Whiteside home, which still looks remarkably similar to its 19th century appearance, was built in 1816 by Alexander Whiteside. Whiteside operated a linen factory in town.

These and many other homes are inextricably linked to the people who have made history in Champlain. As such, many of the photographs in this chapter are identified simply by the names of the residents who once called them home.

Perry's Mills was known as Scheifelins Mills until George Perry purchased full interest in the mills in 1819. Perry had come to the county in 1800 and settled in Mooers before moving east and getting involved in the sawmill and gristmill business. The house was sold to the Kaufman family in the 1880s. The Perry-Kaufman house is still standing on Perry's Mills Road.

This early 1900s image shows the Marshall Maynard home on Main Street adjacent to the bridge. Eventually the home was expanded and used as Noah LaFountaine's store, then Coulombe's store. It is currently being used as a residence again.

Members of the McLellan family (from left to right) Charles, Elizabeth, Hugh, and Malcolm, pose on the steps of the Pliny Moore house in the summer of 1886. Built in 1801 by Pliny Moore, the house was later acquired by Charles McLellan around 1881. His wife Elizabeth was the great-granddaughter of Pliny Moore. The house shown here burned down in 1912 and was rebuilt to the same outside specifications as the original. In the mid-1930s, the McLellans leased the main house to the Clark Funeral Home and moved into the back "cottage." After Woody and Hulda McLellan died in the early 1980s, the house was bought by the funeral home. The Adirondack chair on the steps is now at the Clinton County Historical Association in Plattsburgh.

This Italianate home that still stands on Oak Street is known as the McCrea house for its inhabitants, sisters Elfa McCrea Connell and Elizabeth S. S. McCrea. It currently has a wraparound porch that dramatically alters its appearance. The home has been vacant for a number of years.

A family sits outside the Henry Sanschagrin house in the French Village in this undated photograph. The French Village was a section in the northern part of town that apparently got its name from the many French-speaking families that settled there.

A family relaxes outside the Sanschagrin house.

Two simple frame dwellings on Church Street surround what appears to be a small neighborhood store. The sign affixed to the front of the middle structure is for "Magic Yeast."

A family stands on the porch of their Church Street home.

This brick farmhouse was owned by the Lucas family in Perry's Mills. The *c.* 1900 photograph shows the family on the porch on a winter day. The house burned down in 1948 or 1949. The barns burned down a few years later.

William Dubois Sr. rakes outside his home on Dubois Road in Perry's Mills in this 1948 picture. His wife Clara is in the doorway. The farm, which sits on the banks of the Great Chazy River, has been maintained by the Dubois family for over 135 years.

The Timothy Hoyle house stands on a lot that previously held the first permanent Presbyterian church in Champlain. The brick church was constructed in 1829 and was set on fire by an arsonist in 1844. The Hoyle house was built between 1844 and 1848. The "gingerbread" woodwork at the roof eaves was typical of Gothic Revival houses that were very popular from the 1830s to the 1860s. The house, on the corner of Oak and Chestnut Streets, looks much the same today.

A family sits on the porch of the Bodette House on Perry's Mills Road in Perry's Mills while their horse and buggy stand ready on the side.

Four women in white Victorian gowns pose with the man of the house and the family dog at the Seaman house in Perry's Mills.

Dewey Tavern may be the most historic building still standing in Clinton County. Built by Elias Dewey in 1800, the grounds served as a way station for thousands of British soldiers on their march to Plattsburgh in September 1814. On the retreat back from Plattsburgh, wounded British soldiers were strewn across the floors of the main house and outbuildings. This photograph shows the house as it looks today.

This is the Patrie house as it appeared on Moore Street in the French Village around 1900.

This stone house on Route 276 just before the Canadian border dates from approximately 1815, when Canadians first owned it. In 1847, it was purchased by Isaac Bertrand and then changed hands to Freeman Schoolcraft in 1869. It was most recently owned by George Bedard.

Farmer Willie Lewis once owned this house on Route 11. The home is no longer standing, but another house has replaced it on the same site.

P. F. Dunning, a Champlain hardware merchant, lived in this Italianate Villa in the 1860s. This style of construction was used as early as the late 1830s but was most prevalent in the mid-19th century. This house is still standing on Oak Street.

These houses were constructed for use by Sheridan workers. They were originally situated near the plant on Cherry Street. Most were made of brick and no longer exist. One timber-framed structure was moved further up Cherry Street and still exists today. The area around the Sheridan plant was nicknamed "Nebraska" because of its distance from downtown Champlain.

Oscar Bredenberg, one of the founders of the Bredenberg Ski Factory, once owned this house on Oak Street. The factory, located in Champlain, produced high-quality skis, toboggans, and hockey sticks. The second-floor porch has since been enclosed.

George Vischer Hoyle built this Gothic Revival–style house around 1847. Hoyle grew up in Champlain and, in 1840, became a business partner with Freeman and Bartlett Nye. After eight years, the partnership was dissolved and Hoyle became very active in the business of the newly established railroad in 1849. He worked as a director and then as general superintendent until 1866, when he resigned. In 1853, Hoyle was elected to the New York State Assembly. In 1864, the First National Bank of Champlain was organized and Hoyle was elected its first president and held this position until his death in 1872.

A woman stands outside the Finley house on Elm Street in 1898. This house was built prior to 1869 and was once the home of David Finley, a local foundry man. His foundry eventually became Sheridan Ironworks.

The Whiteside home, a federal-style structure with a Palladian window and hipped roof, dates from 1816. Alexander Whiteside was a local linen manufacturer who married a daughter of Champlain founder Pliny Moore. The house is currently owned by the Yelle family. The marker in the foreground commemorates the first school that stood near the site. The school is of historic significance because William Beaumont, a pioneer in physiology research, was the schoolmaster from 1807 to 1810.

This French Second Empire–style house, built about 1865, was home to Royal Corbin Moore. The house is still standing on Chestnut Street (previously called Matilda Street). Royal, who was the son of Champlain founder Pliny Moore, was the town supervisor in Champlain in 1832.

This photograph is labeled simply as the Perry House, Perry's Mills. It may have belonged to George Perry, for whom the hamlet is named, or one of Perry's relatives.

This house on Prospect Street is barely recognizable today as the stone house in this c. 1900 photograph. Originally owned by Pliny Moore, one of the town's founding fathers, the house was built about 1808. Subsequent owners covered the stone facade with a newer surface. The home is currently owned by Allen Racine.

This photograph shows Manny St. John's farmhouse at the corner of Route 9B and Rapids Road in Coopersville as it appeared around 1911. St. John was the town of Champlain highway superintendent for many years. Pictured from left to right are Florence, Margaret, and Clarence "Duke" Jeannette.

Francois Xavier Garrand is seated and Emma (Garrand) Bechard is to his right in this photograph of the Garrand homestead in Perry's Mills.

Members of the Bechard family stand in front of their farmhouse on Route 9B in Coopersville around 1932. Pictured from left to right are Conrad, Rita, Rollen, Hector, Emma, Delima, and Romeo Bechard.

A row of houses along River Street is visible in the foreground, and St. Mary's Convent is at the center of this bird's-eye view of Champlain.

Four

NORTHERN TIER
COMMERCE

As early as the 1860s, 11 general merchants and numerous tradesmen, including furniture dealers, boat builders, jewelers, and lawyers were plying their wares to Champlain residents. Even the hamlets of Perry's Mills and Coopersville boasted their own hotels, carriage makers, and blacksmiths. However, the hub of commercial activity has always been Main Street and the surrounding area. For decades residents strolled the graceful tree-lined streets and shared the latest news with neighbors.

By 1910, the principal industry was Sheridan Ironworks, where over 125 men worked to produce bookbinding machinery, embossing presses, and other equipment for publishers and manufacturers the world over. Sheridan was the largest industrial employer in Champlain until its closure in 1986. It has been said that almost every individual in the world has come in contact with a product that had passed through a Champlain-made Sheridan machine. The boatyard had also become famous in the region for producing first-class canal boats. In 1909, the boatyard constructed the boats for a floating island that was used during the tercentenary celebration of the exploration of Lake Champlain by Samuel De Champlain that year.

In the late 1920s, a thriving chamber of commerce was proclaiming the beauty of Champlain to a wide audience of potential residents and visitors. A brochure produced at the time proclaimed, "Champlain offers the hospitality of two excellent hotels and a commodious new tourist inn, and various restaurants cater to your needs, at reasonable rates . . . And in the Great Chazy River, which flows through the town, muskellunge fishing is an attraction for sportsmen." The town also prided itself on having one of the largest nurseries dedicated to the propagation of peonies in the state.

Main Street continued to be home to much of Champlain's commercial life until interstate Route 87 was constructed, connecting the region with Albany to the south and Canada to the north. The highway had the effect of bypassing Main Street as a thoroughfare between Plattsburgh and Montreal. Without traffic, the business district on Champlain's Main Street slowly declined.

This impressive Gothic structure was built in 1850 by George Perry. Local tradition has it that Perry imitated the flaring roofline he admired on a trip to Europe. Known as Kaufman's store, it has been a focal point in Perry's Mills for many generations. William "Joe" Dubois, a longtime resident, remembers that people from across the border in Canada and local residents would

often congregate around the potbellied woodstove that sat in the middle of the store. Local boys would hang around to listen to the stories being traded by old-timers. In the 1930s, the store sold penny candy, nails, shoes, salt pork, and any other staples of country life.

In this undated photograph of the interior of Doolittle's store, women's clothing is mixed with other dry goods. Walter H. Doolittle advertised stock that included Natural Bridge shoes, Allen A underwear, and Gordon hosiery.

The machines produced in this factory were used to bind books, produce corrugated cardboard cartons, and shape airplane metal panels, among other uses, and made Sheridan products the standard equipment in many industries. The first structure was built on the site in 1854, and the foundry changed names numerous times before becoming Sheridan Ironworks in the late 1880s. In 1964, the name changed to Sheridan Company, and in 1985 changed again to AM International. In 1986, all operations of AM International were transferred out of state and 700 jobs were lost at the Champlain plant. The buildings are now used by the Kimpex Company of Canada.

The Champlain Tannery was located on Water Street (once called Distillery Street). It was originally built as a distillery in 1811. By 1862, the tannery was operated by Cyrus Savage. It was later operated under the names Hoyle and Huntington, and Isaac D. Porcheron. This photograph depicts the tannery ruins in August 1896.

This 1925 photograph depicts another structure that was part of Sheridan Ironworks. It is labeled "Machine Shop, Champlain, NY, September 15, 1925, J.R. Wiles – builder."

The Gregoire family is well represented in this 1954 photograph inside Sheridan Ironworks. Pictured in the front row, from left to right, are Marcel Gregoire, Frances Dumas, Emile Gregoire, Gerard Gregoire, Leo Gregoire, and Honorius Gregoire. Marcel, Emile, Gerard, and Leo are brothers, and Honorius is their father. Ed Grimshaw is third from left along the back wall, and Alvin Matott is to the far right.

At lunchtime one day in 1938, Emmett Dame remembers that all the employees at Sheridan were asked to come out on the lawn and pose for this photograph. Sheridan Ironworks was the largest employer in town, and, once employed, most workers stayed on the job until retirement. Several residents have been identified in this picture including Bennet Dame, Emmett's brother, (first row), Lockwood Clark, (second row), Oscar Bredenberg, Tom Nicholson, and John Zurlo.

A man stands atop a concrete smokestack under construction in this early photograph of the Sheridan Ironworks.

The Champlain House Hotel was built in 1850 and remained in business until the 1970s when it was converted to office space and apartments. Fire destroyed the building in August 2003.

The Surburban Transport Company delivers patrons down Main Street in Champlain in this photograph. Motorbus service through the Surburban Transport Company began in April 1913, when a car began making trips between Plattsburgh and Rouses Point via Beekmantown Corners, West Chazy, Sciota, Mooers Junction, and Champlain. The service was offered through summer, fall, and as far into winter as road conditions permitted. Both freight and passengers were welcome with a maximum seating capacity of 42.

Noah A. Gload is pictured here in his store on Main Street that had a small butcher shop. He also sold tires, salted peanuts, soap, coffee, tea, and other assorted sundries.

This photograph depicts the intersection of Oak and Elm Streets between 1880 and 1905. The bank building, constructed in 1880, had a second story added in 1905. The structure had been vacant for decades when it was purchased in 2003 by Celine Paquette for use as a local history center. It previously had housed the First National Bank of Champlain, Irona Creameries, and the town's library, where Malcolm McLellan was the librarian.

Pictured here is W. C. LaFountain dry goods store around the beginning of the 20th century. The store was known as the Bon Marche and eventually became Kaufman's. From left to right are Moss Graves, Walter Duquette, and Andrew LaFountain among piles of clothing. Men's suspenders are hanging overhead.

From left to right, Andrew LaFountain, Moss Graves, William LaFountain, and Walter Draquette stand behind a counter at the Bon Marche. Jewelry, pocket watches, and glass bride's baskets are in the glass display case.

Many older residents will remember when the A&P grocery store was housed in the structure identified as Champlain Hall. In this 1920s photograph, the space is occupied by dry goods dealers Wiley and Bertrand, and F. M. Strickland. The signs in the window indicate that Strickland sold clothing, furnishings, trunks, and valises, among other things. The Masonic hall was located on the second floor of this building for many years. The building to the left housed the post office on the first floor and a photography studio on the second floor. The sign in front of the photographer's shop advertises Edison phonographs and records for sale.

Seen here is the interior of Paine's photography studio. The three windows have the same shape as those on the second and third floors of the building in the previous image. R. F. Paine was probably the photographer at that location.

This Main Street image from around 1915 shows four gentlemen outside of William Broder's hardware store, which later became Ralph Lewis's hardware store. Down the street from the hardware store is "Miss M. St. Jean, Milliner." The sign on the tree on the far right of the image reads, "Ice Cream, Cold Drinks and Sandwiches."

These two establishments on Main Street may date from the early 1860s. A tinsmith named Wilson Graves appears in Champlain in the 1862 *Gazetteer*, and a business called Graves and Son is located at the corner of Second and Main Streets next door to a grocery store in the 1869 atlas of Clinton County. In this photograph, Graves and Son is next to a grocery store owned by A. L. Webb. The signs hung around Graves urge their potential shoppers, "Don't go home until you have seen what 5 cents in cash will buy." Also, note the streetlamp between the two shops. By 1888, there were 12 gasoline and 20 kerosene streetlamps installed on Main Street. Louis Louiselle, the first lamplighter in the village, was appointed for $36 a year.

The Savoy,
Champlain, N.Y.

Pictured here is Locust Hill Mansion, later known as the Savoy. Bartlett Nye began construction on the Locust Hill Mansion in 1851. His home, which he called the "Villa at Champlain," was part of an estate that included several outbuildings and gardens. The Nyes were a successful business family, and the home was decorated in high style with 35 mahogany doors, a central staircase of mahogany and ivory, marble fireplaces, and beautiful furnishings. In 1930, the house was converted into a hotel bar and restaurant, called the Savoy, and was operational into the early 1980s. In the late 1980s, the building housed apartments. It burned down on February 18, 2003.

Pictured here, the Champlain Carriage Repository, or shop, advertises "fine carriages, sleighs, harness and saddlery, horse clothing, robes, blankets and whips, and Montana buffalo robes and coats."

A small boy stands out in front of the L. E. Peryer Store on Main Street. The side of the store has advertisements for several plug tobacco brands including Compass A, Wild Fruit, Old Honesty, and Cubanola.

This photograph of the Lyceum Theatre probably dates to around 1930. The poster out front advertises the movie *Chasing Rainbows*, starring Bessie Love, Charles King, and Jack Benny. The theater was at this location from 1914 to 1948. The *Moorsfield Press*, operated by Hugh McLellan and later his son Woody, was in the basement from around 1920 to the early 1980s. The structure, originally the Session House, was built as a temporary meeting space by the Presbyterians after their church was destroyed by fire in 1844. Currently the building houses the Knights of Columbus.

The *Gazetteer* for Franklin and Clinton Counties for 1862–1863 provides a wealth of information about the businesses that operated in small towns throughout both counties. Among the many businesses, from ambrotypist (an early type of photographer) to hairdresser, Champlain had three physicians, two dentists, and three saloons. This advertisement is for general merchant James M. Burroughs. Burroughs was also a partner in a local iron foundry.

James and Alexander Forbes operated one of the furniture stores in town in the early 1860s. Their advertisement in the *Gazetteer* offered the sort of furnishings that were necessary for any finely appointed Victorian home. Gilt mouldings, oil paintings, and horsehair sofas were offered for prices "lower than can be bought at retail in any city."

The Costello Block in the village of Champlain contained the Commercial House and several residences. Located across the street from the Presbyterian church (village hall), the building was originally a hotel called the Mansion House. The Costello Block burned sometime during the 1940s.

The Mansion House hotel, later known as the Costello Block, was in business as early as 1869. It was located at the corner of Main and Church Streets and advertised that "guests conveyed to and from the depot free of charge, also a good livery stable and billiard room connected with the house." This photograph shows, from left to right, Mrs. Napoleon Gamache, her two daughters, Delphis Duquette, and Napoleon Gamache. They visited the hotel around 1896.

This c. 1900 image of Main Street includes Champlain Hall on the right and a barbershop on the left (note the barber pole on the side of the building). It also provides another great look at the stately elm trees along both sides of the road.

The railroad depot in Champlain was constructed in the 1850s by the Northern Railroad. Shortly after it was built, service began from Ogdensburg to Rouses Point. The beautiful Victorian-style architecture complimented the other homes and businesses in the neighborhood. In the early 1880s, the Ogdensburg and Lake Champlain Railroad took control of the station and opened up travel to New England via a bridge over Lake Champlain. The value of Champlain's milk and butter products doubled as they could now be transported to huge markets in Boston. The station burned in the 1960s, and the only remaining vestige is a 1917 freight house, located a few hundred feet from the old station on Chestnut Street. It has since been converted into an apartment building.

The Champlain Creamery on River Street is shown in this picture from around 1900. Farmers are seen delivering their milk in large cans by horse-drawn wagon. A 1910 news article noted that "Champlain has the distinction of being one of the most important milk stations on the Rutland Railway, the Champlain Creamery is doing a very large business."

William Broder, William Paquette, Henry LaFontaine, and Robert Bestor are gathered inside William Broder's hardware store. Note the poster in the lower left-hand corner announcing the celebration for St. Jean Baptiste Day on Wednesday, June 24. One of the main advertised events is a baseball game between Malone and Champlain.

This close-up of the interior of William Broder's hardware store features some of the items for sale in his Main Street establishment, such as keys, hinges, hooks, and paint samples.

A 1914 photograph of the interior of Wiley and Bertrand's dry goods store displays ribbon, fabric, ready-made dresses, and notions. Weary shoppers could even perch on one of the upholstered stools in front of the display cases.

Mr. and Mrs. Robert Wiley stand on either side of their son Leon in this 1885 picture. Leon Wiley later became Henry Bertrand's partner in the dry goods business Wiley and Bertrand.

Tremblay Auto Sales on Main Street was one of the largest car dealerships in northern New York. Arsene Tremblay owned the business and was also the mayor of the village from 1926 to 1943. The building now houses the village offices.

A thriving boatyard was once located at the foot of River Street. This boat was constructed in the Champlain boatyard around the beginning of the 20th century. Champlain-built canal boats were highly valued and known for their easy handling on Lake Champlain. The last known canal boat to come up the Great Chazy River into the village of Champlain was owned by Joseph Allard. It was anchored north of Bill Earl's bicycle repair shop in 1958 and rotted away over time.

In this photograph, the Amos J. Senecal canal boat from Champlain docks at an unknown location. Senecal had two daughters, Margaret and Grace, who probably spent time on this boat. Another Champlain resident from a canal boat family, Louise (Lafountain) Chevalier remembers traveling the Quebec City–to–New York route on her father's boat. John Lafountain took along his family, including two cats, as he transported lumber and coal from early spring until October. Louise remembers missing several months of school each year because of the long canal boat season.

Amos J. Senecal's "war zone pass" was issued by the U.S. Customs Service in December 1917.

Margaret and Grace Senecal ran the Cut-Rate Store on Main Street in the 1930s and 1940s. They sold ice cream, drinks, souvenirs, and novelty items. Doris Picard, a longtime Champlain resident, remembers Margaret as a friendly and talkative woman who always wore her hair tucked neatly in a bun. As a young girl, Picard purchased her supply of alleys (big marbles often used as shooters) from the Cut-Rate Store.

Margaret and Grace Senecal man the counter inside the Cut-Rate Store.

Hogge's Drug Store on Main Street is featured in this undated photograph. Note the old Texaco fuel pumps on the far left.

Bill and Nellie Hogge stand outside their drugstore in Champlain in 1940.

Main Street in Champlain looked much different in the 1940s than it does today. Newer model cars from the 1940s and an old Model T are parked in what was a once a busy commercial area. On the right is the H. W. Falcon store. Down the street a little further is the Rexall Drugstore. The Falcon store building is one of a handful of historic buildings that still stands on Main Street today.

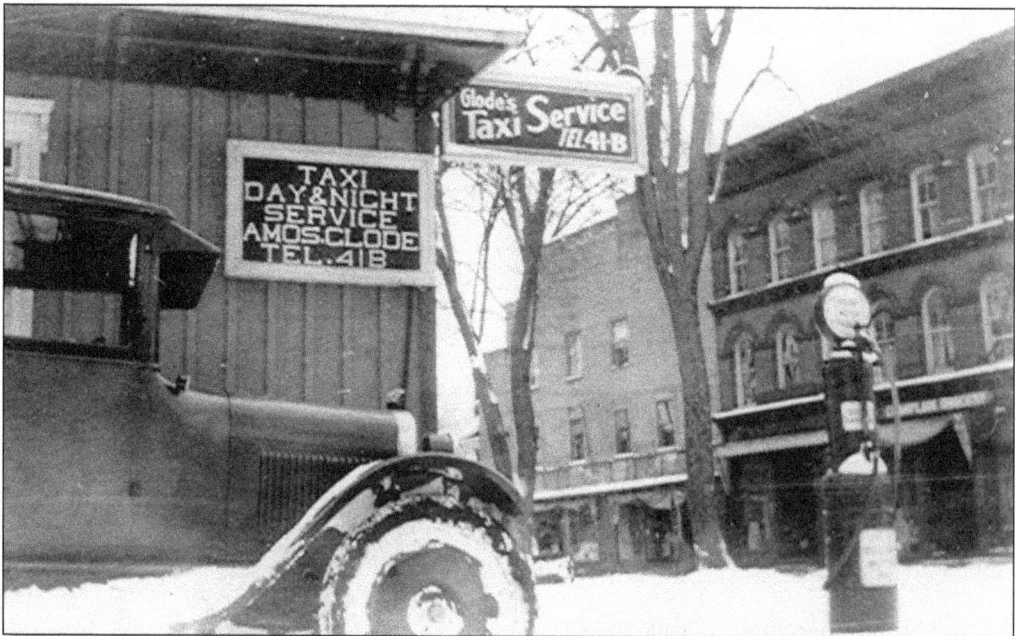

A winter shot of Main Street captures Amos Glode's Taxi Service.

The New York Bargain Store is featured prominently in this 1940 image of Main Street. Phil Agel owned and managed the store for many years. He sold men's and women's clothing, shoes, wallpaper, and other household goods. W. H. Doolittle's store is to the right of the Bargain Store, and at the far left is the A&P and Grand Union.

A young man works the register in this 1950s interior shot of Kaufman's store in Perry's Mills.

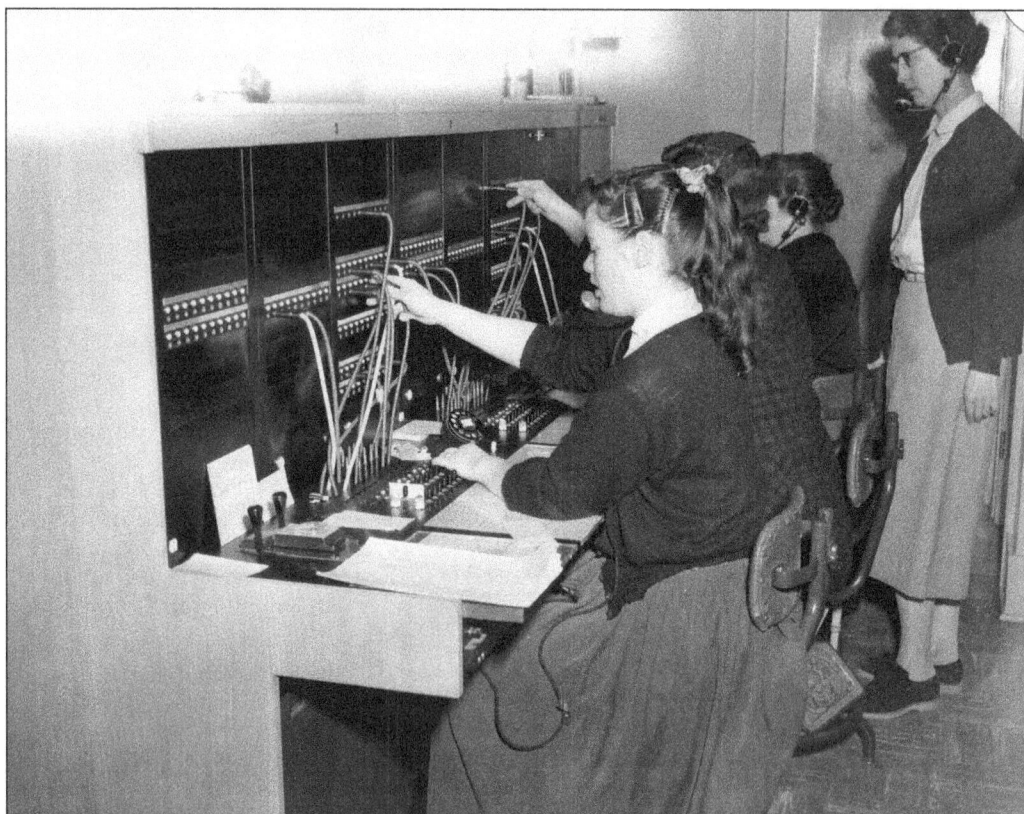

The Champlain Telephone Company has been the local, independent source of communication since its founding in 1903 by Orrin Southwick and Maurice Knapp. It is still primarily a family-run business with third- and fourth-generation family members actively involved in the company. In this photograph, a young telephone operator assists with placing a call.

Joe and Lucienne Lafountain operated the Maple Inn Restaurant and Cabins on Route 9 in Champlain. The inn, seen in this aerial photograph, opened in 1952 and closed in 1982.

Four

IN THE COUNTRYSIDE

While the village was often a bustling center of commerce, the town was carved into many farms, which formed the backbone of the local economy. Champlain had over 225 farms operating in 1862. Like most of 19th-century America, farming and outdoor pursuits comprised the better part of a typical resident's day.

Before 1900, respite from a hard day's work could be found at McCrea's International Fair and Trotting Grounds, and Island Park. Both destinations have long since been abandoned, but the island once hosted speakers, picnics, weekly band concerts, and dances. The fair and trotting grounds featured horse racing, cattle shows, and fair amusements. Both provided an escape from the everyday life of a farmer on the northern frontier.

Life on a farm could be challenging and exhausting, especially given the unforgiving weather of the Northeast. A local paper printed a humorous anecdote about the demanding nature of farm life in the 1930s.

> A worried looking farmer drove to Champlain recently and headed for the family doctor. Without preamble he began:
> 'Doc, the first time you're out my way I wish you'd stop in and see my wife.'
> 'Is she ill?' asked the doctor.
> 'Not exactly.'
> 'What's the trouble then?'
> 'Well, this morning she got up at the regular time, about 4 o'clock; milked the cows, got breakfast for the hands, did her housework; churned, and mopped the kitchen floor. Along about 11 o'clock she said that she was feeling a little tired and I'm worried about her. Maybe she needs a tonic or something.'

A farmer and his weary wife could find support among their peers in the Grange, a fraternal organization that supported agriculture in small rural communities. The Champlain Grange was organized on December 8, 1899, with John Pettinger as the first master and William C. Lewis as the secretary.

After many decades as the social and professional center of the agricultural community, the Champlain Grange dissolved in 1997, following a decline in farming. Farming still continues as a way of life in Champlain, but on a much smaller scale than during previous generations.

Anna Gooley LaFountain and a small friend stand in the doorway of the sugar house on the LaBounty farm on Dubois Road in Perry's Mills. The Gooley home was across the road from the LaBounty farm.

This photograph was taken at LaValley's sugar bush in 1916. It identifies the two people as "Aunt Liza and Freeman." Local residents may recall the North Country tradition of "sugar on snow," which is made when fresh maple sugar is drizzled over snow and hardens into a tasty treat.

This undated photograph was probably taken on the Dubois farm on Dubois Road in Perry's Mills. The farmer on the far right with the pitchfork is Napoleon Dubois. Many farmers eked out livings on small subsistence farms outside the village. The poor condition of the horses in this picture speaks volumes about the hardships that farmers faced.

An 80-ton straw stack is featured in this image of the Laurin farm on Lake Shore Road in Champlain. On the stack are Walter Laurin, Cecile and Pauline Laurin, and their father Paul Laurin. Anthime Laurin is standing at the bottom right of the stack with his brother Emile.

This 1898 portrait of the LaRoche family at their farmhouse proudly displays a spinning wheel, a high chair, and several chairs. It was common for people to bring out their most prized possessions for photographs, as photographs were still a rare occurrence in rural areas at this time.

Four men pose outside the river station in Perry's Mills. From left to right are Francis St. Andrews, Cyril Baker, unidentified, and Willie Baker. The station, which has been in place since 1928, is used to monitor water flow in the Great Chazy River.

In this photograph, a group of men pose, with several holding baseball bats, in front of the Jim Tallman house on Creek Road in Perry's Mills.

Peter Cardin pitches hay at McLellan's border farm on Meridian Road (formerly Oak Street). The border farm was later owned by Allen Racine.

In this photograph, a farmer at McLellan's border farm is seen with a team of horses pulling a seed drill. Before 1900, most farmers used a broadcast method of seed distribution. The seed drill ploughed furrows into which a seed was dropped. This process was followed by a series of presses (metal discs) that covered over the trench.

Rose Dubois (left) of Perry's Mills picks grapes with two unidentified individuals, possibly her parents, in this picture taken around 1900.

A group of men and women gather on the shore of the Great Chazy River.

Willie Lewis and his brother Ralph raised purebred Ayrshire cattle in this barn on Route 11. Most of the dairy farmers in the area raised Holsteins. Ayrshires were known for their rich milk.

A family works outside their rough, log home in Champlain.

Genevieve Gload holds a black lamb in front of the Ashline farm on Rapids Road.

Mary Follens Pelkey stands in the center of this group photograph that was probably taken on the Pelkey farm. Mary and her sister Catherine emigrated from Ireland with their family during the height of the Irish potato famine. By the middle of the 19th century, there were many Irish immigrants living in Champlain and Clinton County. Both sisters settled down with local farmers and raised large families.

Robert McCrea owned the International Fair Grounds and Trotting Park that existed at the same site where the Northway Theatre later operated. This photograph, labeled the Champlain Fairgrounds, is probably McCrea's Park. In the fall of 1878, the International Agricultural Society hosted its first annual fair at the site. Horseracing, animal displays, and a baseball game were scheduled activities. The trotting park side of the operation appears to have been quite busy, as harness races occurred on a regular basis. A race in August 1883 pitted Lady Patsy (owned by Abare and Richards) against White Oak (owned by McCrea and Bosworth). Racing was conducted in one-mile heats with a purse of $225.

Lawrence Ashline sits on a tractor outside his barn on Route 9 in Champlain with two women in this 1953 photograph. The farm, still at the corner of Routes 9 and 11, once belonged to Ashline's aunt, Permelia Ashline Paquette.

The large island in the middle of the Great Chazy River above the bridge was a favorite spot for town events as early as 1807. In 1877, Island Park was a destination for band concerts, picnics, and social events. An office, bathhouse, conservatory, bandstand, and fountains were constructed for the enjoyment of all. Bridges connected both the large and small island with the shore at several points. A dance pavilion was also built on the small island. A news article from the summer of 1883 proclaimed, "Remember county citizens, that we have an Island Park which alone excels any natural attraction in this vicinity."

The main bridge connecting Island Park with Oak Street remained for many years, but constant flooding caused the removal of most of the structures. Mignon cottage, shown in this photograph from Cloak Island, was actually the conservatory that was removed from Island Park. However, even after many of the buildings were gone, the island was still used for events, and electric lights were installed in May 1901.

Several officers of the Champlain Grange Chapter No. 833 wear their insignia in this photograph from the 1930s. The Grange was established in Champlain by 18 charter members in December 1899. It was both a business and a social organization in this primarily agrarian community. Pictured from left to right are (first row) Inez Forgette, Gordon McCrea, Evelyn Clark, Ernest Mellon, and William McCrea; (second row) George Lafountain, Mary McCrea, Nancy Ashline, William Dubois, Jacob Ashline, Pearl Deso, Hershey Deso, Edna Favreau, Alex Sterns, Clara Ashline Dubois, and Lawrence Ashline.

Two children with a carriage pose in front of machinery being used to construct Perry's Mills Road in Perry's Mills. The small brick structure in the background is the Perry's Mills schoolhouse.

This photograph is labeled "Papa and I with a load of hoops for Tom Lewis." Papa is Hector Kaufman Sr. and the son is Hector Kaufman Jr. The Kaufman's were in the barrel-making business along with the operation of a general store in Perry's Mills.

Clara St. John holds her niece Viola St. John Lucas, and stands next to another niece, Marion St. John Bechard, in front of their home in 1925. Many farming implements are scattered about the yard.

This photograph depicts Maurice, Lester, and Clara Ashline on the Ashline family farm on Rapids Road. The Ashline farm was established in the early 19th century by descendants of the first settler to the town of Champlain, Prisque Asselin (Ashline).

Five

A CLOSE-KNIT COMMUNITY

The Champlain community has always been composed of a diverse mix of people from different ethnic backgrounds. Whether English, French, Irish, or Scottish, a common identity has been forged through the local schools, churches, and community organizations that serve them all. This chapter looks at those organizations, including the Champlain Fire Department, that have been a focal point for community interaction.

A great tradition of community spirit rose from the Depression of the 1930s, as a series of "community exhibits" were put on by the village every October for seven straight years. According to event organizers, the community exhibits were created to advertise Champlain, boost local business, and help the citizens of Champlain become more acquainted with one another. While only one or two photographs have surfaced to document this tradition, there are printed event programs that detail the myriad of events that took place. The Grange Chorus put on a skit one year and sang "It's Good to Be a Granger!" Other organizations, including the literary club and students at local schools, took part in the entertainment as well. Ultimately it was the success of the community exhibits that led to their demise. Over the years, attendance rose from 1,400 the first year to over 5,000 in the last year. Village officials were concerned that the crowds were becoming excessive and thus cancelled the annual event.

Community togetherness is clearly still alive and well in Champlain. The ice storm in the winter of 1998 was a testament to the willingness of Champlain residents to help one another in times of need. The storm tested the resolve of the community like no other recent event. The town and its citizens came through with great success. Neighbor helped neighbor, and local organizations, including the fire department, public works crews, utility crews, and the telephone company, performed admirably during a time of great crisis.

Champlain Academy students are pictured in front of the school about 1923. In the photograph are (first row) Maxwell G. Orr, Betty McCrea, Rachel Stone, Edith Kaufman (Knapp), Evelyn Greenwood, Kenneth C. Kaufman, Pearl E. Trombly, unidentified, Raymond Stone, Kermit Plummer, Richard Dudley, Roger H. Lucas, and Merrill E. Ives; (second row) Elfa McCrea, Bertha Gokey, Eleanor A. Coonan, Margaret Kennedy, Kathryn L. Falcon, Dorothy Laventure, Alma E. Linder, Charis J. Sunderland, George Bateman, Charles W. McLellan, and Clifford M. Seaman; (third row) Professor Marvin, ? King, Claudia A. Lafontaine, Lucille Southwick, Ruth Dudley, Katherine Bateman, Harley Webb, Francis J. Falcon, and Malcolm D. McCrea.

Miss Lucas is the teacher presiding over this class of first- and second-grade children in the Champlain Union Free School for the 1921–1922 academic year. From left to right are (first row) Richard Phaneuf, Chester Lavalley, ? Deso, Richard Kennedy, Billy Eldrid, and Andrew Sunderland; (second row) Erika Clark, Albert Robinson, Alfred Walling, Raymon Cardin, Myron Jackson, and Lawrence Ashline; (third row) Benet Dame, Dorothy Elvidge, Lida Cardin, Madeleine Phaneuf, Deal Mason, and Naoma Mellon.

This 1907 image depicts a one-room schoolhouse on Tallman Road in Perry's Mills. The schoolhouse has since been demolished, and a residence now stands in its place.

Maude Dudley presides over a classroom decorated for Halloween. The date on the blackboard reads October 26, 1954. Dudley taught at local schools for many years and was much beloved by her students. The elementary school, on Elm Street, was formerly Champlain Central School.

About 40 children stand outside a school building with their teacher (back center) in this 1918 photograph of the Perry's Mills School.

The original high school in Champlain was erected in 1842 and was called the Champlain Academy. The building pictured here cost $11,000 to build after the academy was destroyed by fire in 1887. This structure also burned to the ground in December 1940. A third building was constructed on Elm Street by architect Hugh McLellan to replace the high school. The building is now vacant.

Champlain Academy smolders after the fire in 1940.

Members of the Champlain Fire Department relax at a dinner at the Savoy in this *c.* 1950 picture. Standing in the back are, from left to right, Alfred Sonnie Babbie, Bennet Dame, Jack Vallee, Paul Cumberland, Hunk Degenhardt, Ernest Hamel, Claude Lavoie, Myron Zeke Dengenhardt, Larry Jarvis, Charlie Southwick, Arthur Lapline, Lester Hamel, Girard Juneau, Al Glaude, Roger Tetrault, Armand Cardin, Francis Dumas, Jim Todd, Jimmy Glaode, Charlie Chevalier, and Roger Dupre (seated against side wall). Leo Monette is seated at the head of the right-side table. Frankie Monette is seated at the front of the right table, and behind him, moving around the inside of the two tables are, Leon Snoot Trombley, Jimmy Chevalier, Clifford Laplante, Stewart Reed, Frank Hamel, Bob Dumont, Emile Gregoire, Stevens Johnson, Orrin Higgins, and Kenneth Laplante (front, left table). The two gentlemen seated on the far left are Carl and Aurel Parsons.

Champlain purchased its first fire wagon in 1873. The word Niagara, derived from the manufacturer, is painted on the side. The Champlain volunteer fire department adopted its present name, Niagara Hose Company, No. 1, based on this first piece of equipment. The wagon was lined with copper so that it could be filled with water. Sixty men were needed to fully man it. The Niagara pumper remained in service until 1933, when the department was given a 1918 American LaFrance.

The town of Champlain received this brand-new truck in 1948 from the General Fire Truck Corporation in Detroit. It was capable of showering 750 gallons of water per minute. (Photograph by Michael Costello.)

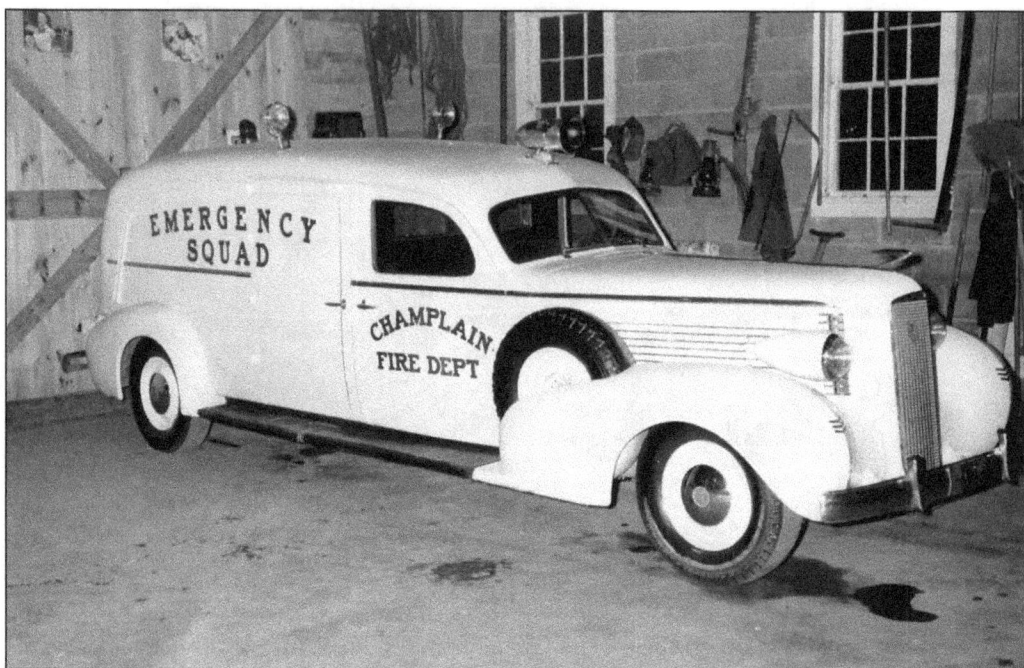

Once used as a hearse by the Clark Funeral Home, this 1937 Lasalle was converted to an emergency squad car in 1951 by members of the fire department.

In this photograph, members of Niagara Hose Company No. 1 compete in a "Three Man Ladder" contest at the Clinton County Firemen's Association Convention and Field Day, held at the Champlain Central School grounds on July 25, 1954. Roger Tetrault is at the top of the ladder, Ernest Hamel is second, and Francis Dumas Jr. is third. The official timers at the top of the platform are, from left to right, Smith Labarre, Chazy Fire Department; Daniel Maher, principal of Champlain Central School; and Arthur Forkey, Mooers Fire Department.

The Champlain Fire Department band plays on the deck of a boat in this undated photograph. Members of the current fire department believe that a band existed at one point in the organization's history, but very little is known about it.

One of only two photographs that have been found of the community exhibits, this image depicts a crowd gathered for a show. It was taken on October 17, 1935, by M. L. Wright.

The Presbyterian church building has a long history in Champlain. The Congregational Presbyterian church was first organized in Champlain in July 1802. Situated on the corner of Church and Main Streets, the structure was built in 1849 and had a belfry with an 800-pound bell. Its Greek Revival design, with Ionic columns at the entrance and a gable end, was typical for the time. The belfry and much of the tower was ruined in a 1927 fire. The church was rebuilt after the fire and was used as village hall until a few years ago. It is currently vacant.

Firefighters battle a hopeless cause as the Presbyterian church is gutted by fire on December 4, 1927. The blaze started in the furnace box and within a half hour nothing but the brick walls remained standing. The $35,000 loss was only partially covered by insurance.

Until 1818, Roman Catholic residents of Champlain could only count on sporadic religious services from traveling Canadian priests. After 1818, a rough-hewn log structure across from the present St. Joseph's church may have served as a place of worship until it burned in March 1823. Fr. Victor Dugas came to Coopersville (Corbeau) in 1828 and maintained services until his death in 1844. His replacement, Fr. Louis Lapic, took charge of the parish and the construction of a permanent church that was begun in 1845. When St. Joseph's Church was built (shown here as it appeared around 1900), it was the only Catholic parish north of Plattsburgh.

Pictured here is Fr. A. A. Thomas with two girls outside the rectory at St. Joseph's in Coopersville on August 8, 1896. Father Thomas was born in Perigueux, France, in 1830 and was noted as "a writer of considerable merit," who had published tales of his travels in Europe and America. He served the parish from 1881 to 1896.

In September 1854, the first Episcopal church was constructed in Champlain on the left bank of the river on Moore Street (formerly Oak Street.). St. John's, was officially organized in March 1853 with 90 congregants. It was built of wood in the Gothic style. The church burned down in December 1904 and the current brick church was built in its place. It later became the Presbyterian church.

CHURCH CHAMPLAIN, N.Y.

The first Roman Catholic church in Champlain to bear the name St. Mary's was the old Methodist meeting house on Church Street. The building was purchased in 1859 for $450 and enlarged to 2,100 square feet holding up to 500 parishioners. The present church, located a short distance from the first church, was completed in 1887 under the direction of Fr. Francois X. Chagnon. This photograph of the later structure predates the 1907 installation of the Samuel de Champlain Monument and the stone sacristy.

Altar boys line the front of the church in this undated interior photograph of St. Mary's.

Fr. Francois X. Chagnon, a priest at St. Mary's Church, is sitting in the center of this photograph of young boys from April 1908. The boys' sashes indicate that they are officers in an honor guard.

This building was first the residence of Dr. Hackett before becoming St. Mary's convent and boarding school in 1906. Hackett was remembered for driving his sleigh through all types of weather, covered in bearskins and buffalo robes, to deliver babies and tend to the sick. The convent was operated by the Daughters of Charity of the Sacred Heart of Jesus.

Six

LIFE IN A BORDER TOWN

A community's history is often told through a series of events, both good and bad, that have marked its people and places. Champlain is no different. For years residents have related the past to a certain flood, a major storm, time of war, accidents, or celebrations.

Nature has been the catalyst for many of the area's most memorable events. Snowstorms, ice storms, and floods have plagued this northern outpost of New York for decades. The village's close proximity to the Great Chazy River has made rising water a constant threat. The floods of 1886 and 1911 stand out as particularly harsh, and photographs depict the havoc that water has continually wreaked on residents and businesses.

Train wrecks, fires, and car accidents are some of the man-made disasters that also find their way into this chapter, along with a glimpse of Champlain's French flavor. A traveler to the area in the late 19th century sent a postcard back home that remarked of Champlain, "This is more of a Canadian French village then American." And this was certainly true in many ways. The fervor with which residents celebrated the festival of St. Jean Baptiste attests to its strong connections to its French ancestry. Older generations will remember the annual celebration on June 24, which recognizes the birth of St. John the Baptist. The day has always carried special importance for French Catholics, who brought the tradition to Canada and America.

Another event that celebrated the area's French heritage was the installation of the monument to Samuel de Champlain, the French founder of Lake Champlain. The unveiling of the monument on July 4, 1907, was cause for a huge celebration that proudly proclaimed the ties between France, Canada, and the residents of Champlain.

And, finally, other images help us remember those who braved the uncertainties of war to protect loved ones back home. A monument dedicated on October 9, 1943, once stood outside town hall in recognition of individuals from Champlain who served their country during times of conflict. Unfortunately, the monument has since been removed, and along with it, a tangible reminder of the sacrifices made by these individuals.

The funeral for soldier Armand Catelli was held on November 29, 1919, in this Church Street building. Catelli died as a result of a poison gas attack during World War I. His father, Peter Catelli, stands behind the coffin. The first pall bearer on the right is Ferdinand St. Maxens. The first pall bearer on the left is Douglas Pyper. The undertaker, Elmer Deal, who is not wearing a hat, is standing to the right of the coffin. The soldier on the left front is Peter Gooley, and the third man in is Orville Gload. The sailor is Darcy Coonan. Champlain Post No. 767 of the American Legion was formed a month after this picture was taken.

A military encampment area was set up in the field at the intersection of Moore and Main Streets in the village of Champlain around the time of World War I. This picture may depict activities at that camp. A large military training camp was established in Plattsburgh in 1916 to train business and professional men. Participants would attend four to five weeks of intensive military instruction each year in preparation for active service during times of war.

Men drafted for service in World War I depart for Plattsburgh over the Canada Street (formerly Elm Street) bridge in this September 21, 1917, photograph. Several cars are draped in large American flags, while others have smaller flags attached at their sides.

Over 100 people attended a luncheon at the McCrea residence as part of a town wide celebration in 1959. The festivities included a rededication of the Samuel de Champlain Monument, an exhibit on old Champlain, dedication of a new post office, and a celebration of Champlain's famous son, Jehudi Ashmun. The event attracted a representative from Pres. Dwight D. Eisenhower's staff and a performance by the Andrews Sisters.

Dignitaries line up in front of the Samuel de Champlain Monument at St. Mary's for another official event related to the 1959 celebration. Pictured are, from left to right, Lawrence Paquette, Hubert Papelian, Jack Pettinger, unidentified, John H. G. Pell (chairman of the Lake Champlain Festival), Francis Alphonso (first secretary and counsel of the Embassy of Liberia), and Roger de Champlain.

Children and curious adults inspect the remains of the W. C. LaFountain block in the village of Champlain. The building was gutted by fire on April 12, 1909. It housed a hat shop, a barbershop, and several residences. Leon Poissant, the owner of the hat shop, burned to death after becoming disoriented while trying to salvage some goods. The barber, Louis Charron, and several other families were able to escape before the fire became too severe.

Some 6,000 visitors descended on Champlain for the dedication of the Champlain Monument on July 4, 1907. It was the first erected in the United States to honor Samuel de Champlain. The entire village was decorated for the occasion with American flags and the tri-color of France. The *Champlain Counselor* reported that "American and French citizens united to celebrate an event equally glorious to both nations." The signs on the church read "Vive Champlain" and "Nous nous Souvenons."

The smiling woman in this photograph is wearing a sailor hat marked with "Champlain 1907." She probably participated in the festivities surrounding the dedication of the Samuel de Champlain Monument. Members of many local societies and organizations marched in a grand parade through the principal streets of the village. Many wore sailor costumes to honor one of the greatest navigators of the 17th century.

The 1907 Fourth of July parade makes its way past the Champlain House down Main Street. The parade that year was particularly large because it also commemorated the unveiling of the Samuel de Champlain Monument. However, Fourth of July events were always large affairs. In 1878, almost 9,000 people were reported to have attended the festivities in Champlain.

This Prohibition-era photograph depicts the fate of many rumrunners and revelers as they hit the sharp turn before the bridge off of Oak Street. In his book *Rum Across the Border*, Allan Everest tells of the Saturday night mishaps that were bound to happen as visitors to the Meridian Hotel and nightclub, just over the border in Canada, returned to the United States via the village of Champlain. Everest notes, "Smash-ups occurred with such regularity that, as Woody McLellan comments, 'It got so we would wait up for it because every Saturday night there would be an accident.'" Bootlegging was a fairly big industry in Champlain during Prohibition because of its advantageous location on a main route between Canada and points south.

This photograph shows an ice jam in 1911 near a row of houses on River Street. These houses no longer exist.

High water rises outside the "5 and 10 Ct. Department" in this April 1911 photograph.

A flood stops business at the Bon Marche, owned by W. C. Lafountain, Albert Cayea's grocery store, and a saloon.

In this 1904 photograph, a man finds an alternate form of transportation during a flood. The sign high on the side of the building to the right is for "Severe Legendre, Merchant, Tailor."

Snow is piled high outside the Champlain Hall in this undated photograph. Main Street was often afflicted with the curse of either too much water or too much snow. In March 1900, a series of storms left Champlain blanketed in snow called "the worst known even to the memory of the oldest inhabitant." Harsh winds and thickly falling snow pounded the area for several days. Horses floundered in deep drifts of wet snow, and travel was close to impossible.

The children seen here enjoy Champlain's own version of an iceberg.

121

A fire that started in a building across from Village Hall on April 27, 1912, spread quickly because of high winds, gutted a nearby bakery, crossed the river, and eventually destroyed the McLellan residence (now the Clark Funeral Home) on Elm Street. The McLellan home, known as the Pliny Moore homestead, is at the right in this image. The structure was originally built by Pliny Moore in 1801. The home was later rebuilt in 1913 based on detailed drawings of the original structure made by Hugh McLellan, the owner's son. Seated on the curb at the lower left is longtime Champlain resident Bill LaBelle and his sister Virginia.

In August 1891, a major railroad accident occurred just east of the railway depot. An eastbound mail train collided with a train carrying Sunday school students coming back from an outing. Many were killed including Champlain residents Wilmer Angell, 17, and Henry Lamountagne, 23.

Another image of the 1891 train wreck shows a man outfitted with early diving gear.

A group of boys is perched on the wreckage caused by a 16-car train derailment at the old Route 11 crossing in 1916.

A young woman walks by additional wreckage from the derailment at Route 11.

The St. Jean Baptiste parade travels by the Trepanier and LaFountain grocery store on June 24, 1913. The float in the front of the photograph is sponsored by F. X. Jodoin, harness maker. The wagon behind is decorated with "Champlain" pennants. The festival of St. Jean Baptiste was a point of pride for many French residents. The French Catholic population in Champlain was large enough to support the opening of St. Mary's, a Roman Catholic parish, in 1859. According to the 1990 United States census, one-third of Clinton County residents trace their lineage back to French or French-Canadian ancestry.

Albert Morelli served proudly in the U. S. Navy on the U.S.S. *Thomas Jefferson* and the U.S.S. *Harry Lee* during World War II. Shortly after landing in Sicily in August 1943, he wrote a letter back to his family letting them know that he had, "been in Sicily raising Hades." "You must know all about the invasion by this time and how the troops are taking the Island over. From reports the first wave from our ship was the first to reach the beach, and I was in the first wave. It was a rough night and very dark and I was a little scared when we left the ship and headed for the beach . . . there were lights in every direction – more of them that at any fourth of July celebration that I ever saw. When the sun came up we felt a little better, although we were still under fire and enemy planes were dropping 'eggs' around us." Morelli, who was also in the first wave of soldiers to land at Normandy, is one of a handful of Champlain veterans who are still around to share their experiences. Morelli's story is representative of the experiences of other surviving World War II veterans, including Al Strack, Andrew Juneau, Hector Kaufman, Lockwood Clark, Ernest Lavoie, and Francis Roberts.

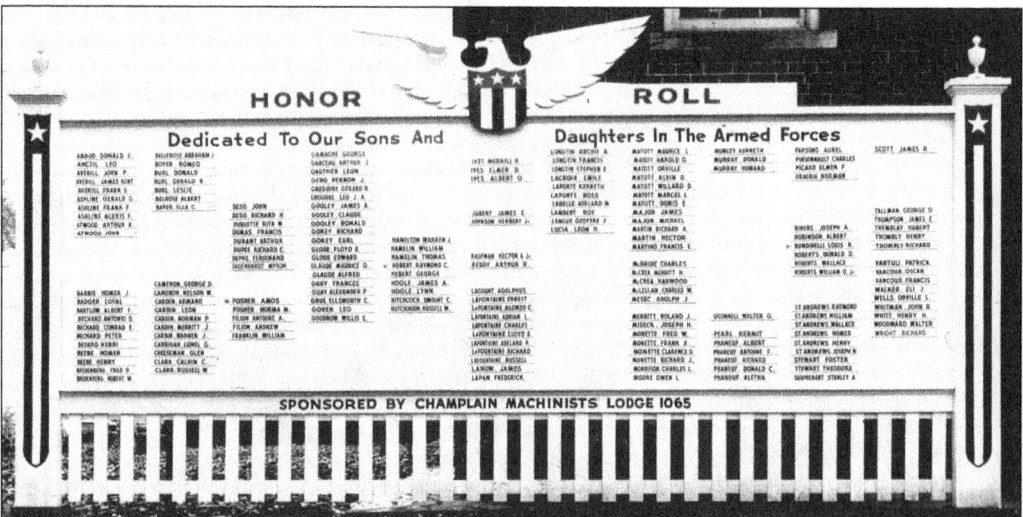

The Champlain Honor Roll, located outside the old town hall, was dedicated to men and women who served in the armed forces. It was sponsored by the Champlain Machinists Lodge 1065 and was dedicated in October 1943. A veiling ceremony was held on October 26, 1947, and a prayer was said for all those soldiers who did not return from battle.

BIBLIOGRAPHY

Atlas of Clinton County, New York. New York, NY: F. W. Beers, A. D. Ellis and C. G. Soule, 1869.

Champlain Counsellor, Champlain, NY.

Everest, Allan S. *Moses Hazen and the Canadian Refugees in the American Revolution.* Syracuse, NY: Syracuse University Press, 1976.

Everest, Allan S. *Our North Country Heritage.* Plattsburgh, NY: Tundra Books, 1972.

Everest, Allan S. *Pioneer Homes of Clinton County 1790-1820.* USA: George Little Press. 1971.

Everest, Allan S. *Rum Across the Border, the Prohibition Era in Northern New York.* Syracuse, NY: Syracuse University Press, 1978.

Gazetteer and Directory of Franklin and Clinton Counties. Ogdensburgh, NY: Advance Office, 1862

Moore, Suzanne E. *The Living Stone: A History of St. Joseph's Roman Catholic Church, Coopersville, NY.* Plattsburgh, NY: Northeast Printing, 1996.

North Countryman, Rouses Point, NY.

Paquette, Lawrence & Charles W. McLellan. *Centennial of the Village of Champlain, New York: Some Historical Notes.* 1973.

Patrick, David. *The Village of Champlain, New York Past and Present: A McLellan Family Perspective.* June 2002.

Plattsburgh Daily Press, Plattsburgh, NY

Plattsburgh Sentinel, Plattsburgh, NY.

Press Republican, Plattsburgh, NY

Town of Champlain 2000. Rouses Point, NY: Border Press, 2000.

Visit us at
arcadiapublishing.com

www.ingramcontent.com/pod-product-compliance
Lightning Source LLC
Chambersburg PA
CBHW080609110426
42813CB00006B/1449